Mother Polar Bear

Written by Sandra Iversen

Mother polar bears
live in the Arctic zone.
Look at the globe.
You can see the Arctic zone.

Where Polar Bears Live

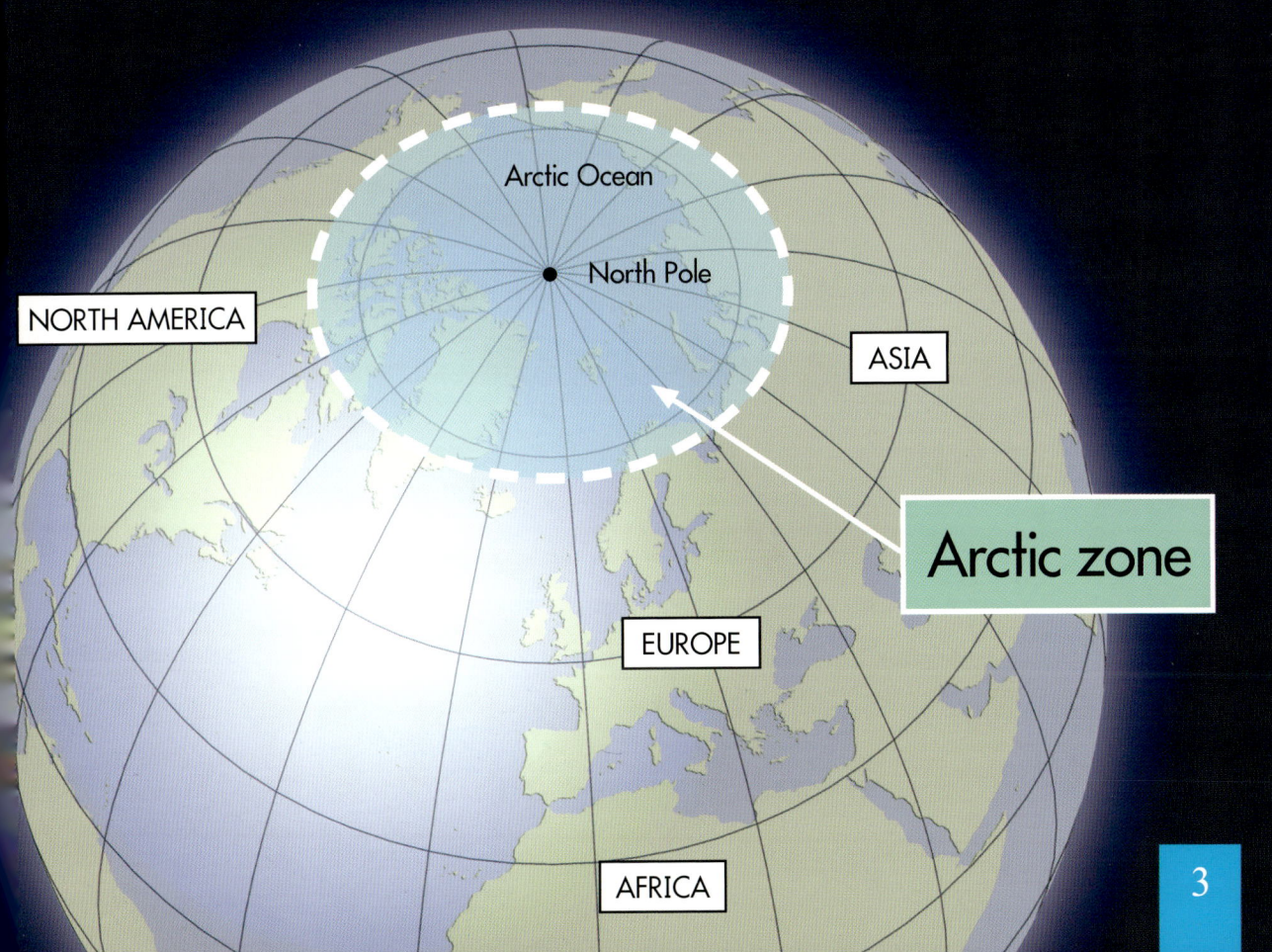

A mother polar bear lives on the ice.
This is her home.
Her home is cold.

A mother polar bear makes a den.
She digs a hole on a slope
for her den.
It is not so cold in the den.
She eats and eats.

She has her cubs in the den.
She does not go out.
She stays in the den with her cubs.

When it is not so cold,
a mother polar bear takes her cubs
out onto the ice.

Now they live out on the ice.